Anthony Benezet

Some Observations on the Situation, Disposition, and Character of the Indian Natives of this Continent

.

Anthony Benezet

Some Observations on the Situation, Disposition, and Character of the Indian Natives of this Continent

ISBN/EAN: 9783337408824

Printed in Europe, USA, Canada, Australia, Japan

Cover: Foto ©Suzi / pixelio.de

More available books at **www.hansebooks.com**

OBSERVATIONS

ON THE

SITUATION, DISPOSITION,

AND

CHARACTER

OF THE

INDIAN NATIVES

OF THIS

CONTINENT.

---

*I will declare the Decree: The LORD hath said unto me,
Thou are my Son, this Day have I begotten thee. Ask of
me, and I shall give thee the Heathen for thine Inheritance, and the uttermost Parts of the Earth for thy Poffeffion.* PSALM ii. 7.

*Open thy Mouth for the Dumb, in the Caufe of all fuch as
are appointed to Deftruction.* PROV. xxxi. 8.

PHILADELPHIA:

PRINTED AND SOLD BY JOSEPH CRUKSHANK, IN
MARKET-STREET.

M DCC LXXXIV.

THE writer of the following sheets has thrown together a few facts, to obviate some mistakes which have been embraced, respecting the Natives of this land; he neither wishes to flatter those of his own colour by acknowledging that they are superior to the tawney Indian; otherwise than as they excel him in acts of beneficence and of an imitation of the the great Author of the Christian Religion; whose name they have assumed; nor to exalt the character of the poor untutored Indian, at the expense of truth, by over-rating their chastity, their love of justice, and hospitality; particularly in their affectionate reception of our Ancestors on their first settlement of Pennsylvania; nor to say more in their favour than is supported by the concurrent testimonies of historians of various religious professions and different nations.

Neither is it intended to justify these people in any of their acts of cruelty:

The

The motives which have induced the writer to engage in this publication are superior to party views; an apprehenfion of duty, and univerfal good-will to mankind. And if the Indian is reprefented to have been oppreffed and injured, it is not to provoke a fpirit of retaliation, nor to excite a difcontent, but to ftate to the view of the public, wherein they have been aggrieved; and wherein they have been culpable, that the people of thefe ftates may fee they have not been free from blame, in hopes that a more candid and indulgent confideration of their fituation may excite in us humanity and tendernefs.

Be not offended therefore if the Indian is reprefented as a rational being as well as ourfelves, if having an immortal foul, capable of receiving the refining influence of our holy religion, it is that he may be allowed to dwell in fafety, and rejoice in the opportunity, which a return of peace, may afford to inftruct him in the knowledge of the true God.

If doubts fhould remain, whether the Indians are, indeed fufceptible of thofe religious impreffions as here mentioned; the reader is referred to the feveral accounts of the fuccefsful labours of the pious

ous Thomas Mayew, John Elliott, and others in New-England, publifhed by themfelves; and alfo a publication of a more late date, by David Brainard, of New-Jerfey who refided among them feveral years, entitled, Mirabila Dei inter Indicos : Or the Rife and Progrefs of a remarkable Work of Grace amongft a Number of Indians, in the Provinces of New-Jerfey and Pennfylvania.

SOME

SOME

OBSERVATIONS

ON THE

INDIAN NATIVES

OF THIS

CONTINENT.

SITUATE as we are on this Continent with very extenſive frontiers, bordering upon a vaſt wildernefs, inhabited by the native Indians, it becomes a ſubject worthy the moſt ſerious attention of every friend of mankind, every lover of his country, to be truly informed what is the ſituation and diſpoſition of that people, ſo far as it may have an influence upon our duty as Chriſtians, and our peace and ſafety as members of Civil Society : And that we may not make a raſh

eftimate

eftimate of our own importance, or of the incapacity of thofe people for religious improvement, the following obfervations and quotations are recommended to the ferious perufal of every reader, as they give a view of the opinions of fome of the early fettlers, of different denominations, in this continent.

The firft fettlers of Pennfylvania, who had full opportunities of being acquainted with the nature and difpofition of the Natives, and who made it a principal point to obferve ftrict juftice in all their tranfactions with them, have left us very favourable memorials of the long continued kindnefs they experienced from thefe people : the great difadvantages to which their ignorance and roving temper fubjected them, our forefathers thought it their duty to endeavour to draw them from, by exemplary acts of benevolence and inftruction ; which pious practice has fince been fuccefsfully purfued, by feveral well difpofed perfons in New-England, New-Jerfey, and elfewhere: feveral of whom have tranfmitted fatisfactory accounts of their labours.

From thefe publications as well as from the remembrance of fome yet living, it is evident, that the natural difpofition of
the

the Indians has generally been to ſhew kindneſs to the Europeans, in their early ſettlements; and that their mental powers are equally with our own capable of improvement; that the apparent differ-. ence in them, as well as in the Black People and us, ariſes principally from the advantages of our education, and manner of life.

Some writers have repreſented Indians as naturally ferocious, treacherous, and ungrateful, and endeavoured to eſtabliſh this character of them, from ſome parti- cular tranſaction which hath happened on ſpecial occaſions: but no concluſion of their original character ſhould be drawn from inſtances in which they have been provoked, to a degree of fury and vengeance, by unjuſt and cruel treatment from European Aggreſſors; of which moſt hiſtories of the firſt ſettlements on this continent furniſh inſtances, and which writers have endeavoured to colour and vindicate, by reprobating the character of thoſe poor people.

It is a matter of fact, proved by moſt Hiſtorical Accounts of the trade carried on with the Indians at our firſt acquaintance with them, as well as in the firſt ſettlements made on this continent, that
they

they generally manifested themselves to be kind, hospitable and generous to the Europeans, so long as they were treated with justice and humanity; but when the adventurers from a thirst of gain, over reached the Natives, and they saw some of their friends and relations treacherously entrapped and carried away to be sold for slaves, * themselves injuriously treated and driven from their native possessions, what could be expected but that such a sordid conduct in the Europeans, would produce a change of disposition in the Indians. The early settlers of New-Jersey have always confirmed the testimony of the Pennsylvanians, with respect to the good usage they met with

---

* Amongst the many instances of this kind which might be given, that are recorded by different authors, the following is most striking, viz. One Hunt an early trader with the Indians of New-England, after a prosperous trade with the Natives, enticed between 20 or 30 on board his vessel. and contrary to the public faith, clapped them under hatches, and f ld them to the Spaniards at Malaga ; but the Indians resented it, and revenged themselves on the next English that came on the coast. Neal's. History of New-England, page 21.

with from the Indians. The writer of
the Hiftory of that Province informs us,
page 440, " That, for almoft a centu-
" ry, the Natives had all along maintain-
" ed an intercourfe of great cordiality
" and friendfhip with the inhabitants."
It is well known that the Indians' de-
portment to each other is peaceable and
inoffenfive; efteeming fudden anger un-
becoming and ignominious; they feldom
differ with their neighbour, or do them
any harm or injury, except when intoxi-
cated by ftrong liquor, of which they are
fond, to an enormous degree: this is the
general charaĉter given of Indians, by all
impartial writers.

The noted French author Charlevoix,
who appears to have been deep in his in-
quiries into their manners and difpofition, in his long travels from Quebec, thro'
the lakes and down the Miffiffipi to Flo-
rida, informs, " That with a mein and
" appearance altogether favage; and
" with manners and cuftoms which fa-
" vour the greateft barbarity, the Indi-
" ans enjoy all the advantages of fociety.
" At firft view, fays he, one would ima-
" gine them without form of govern-
" ment, law or fubordination, and fub-
" ject to the wildeft caprice; neverthe-
" lefs,

" lefs, they rarely deviate from certain
" maxims and ufages founded on good
" fenfe alone, which holds the place of
" law, and fupplies in fome fort, the
" want of legal authority.* Reafon
" alone is capable of retaining them in a
" kind of fubordination; not the lefs
" effectual, towards the end propofed,
" for being entirely voluntary. They
." manifeft much ftability in the engage-
" ments they have folemnly entered up-
" on ; patient in affliction, as well as in
" their fubmiffion to what they appre-
" hend to be the appointment of Provi-
" dence ; in all which they manifeft a
" noblenefs of foul, and conftancy of
" mind, at which we rarely arrive with
" all our Philofophy and Religion. As
" they are neither flaves to ambition, nor
" interest ;

---

* Human Nature, even in its rudeft ftate, is .
poffeffed of a ftrong fenfe of right and wrong ; a
pure principle which is not confined to any name
or form, but diffufes itfelf as univerfally as the
fun; it is " *That light which enlightens every man*
" *coming into the world,*" John i. 9. All thofe
who yield to its impreffions are brethren in the
full extent of the expreffion, however differing in
other refpects.

" intereſt ; the two paſſions which have
" ſo much weakened in us thoſe ſenti-
" ments of humanity, which the kind
" Author of Nature has engraven in the
" human heart, and kindled thoſe of co-
" vetouſneſs, which are as yet generally
" unknown amongſt them."

Is it not notorious that they are generally kinder to us than we are to them?
There is ſcarce an inſtance occurs, but
that they treat every white man, who
comes amongſt them, with reſpect;
which is not the caſe from us to them.

Their modeſt conduct to women who
have been captured by them, is certainly
worthy of commendation, much exceeding what would be expected, in like
caſes, from the lower claſs amongſt ourſelves.

It is alſo acknowledged by all impar-
tial perſons, who have been converſant
with Indians, that they have generally
manifeſted a faithfulneſs to the engagements they have entered into for the ſafety of any perſon they have undertaken to
protect, far exceeding that to be found
amongſt the generality of white people;
as alſo in the performance of thoſe cove-
nants which they have confirmed by giving belts of wampum.

Charlevoix

Charlevoix farther obferves, " That
" whoever infinuates himfelf in their
" efteem, will find them fufficiently do-
" cile to do any thing he defires ; but
" that this is not eafily gained, as they
" generally give it to merit only, of
" which they are as good judges as moft
" amongft us. He adds, that thefe good
" difpofitions are very much eclipfed by
" the cruelty they fometimes exercife
" upon fuch of their enemies, whom
" they have devoted to death ; as well as
" the right they almoft univerfally claim
" to private revenge. They confider it
" as a point of honour to avenge inju-
" ries done to their friends, particular-
" ly the death of a relation ; blood for
" blood, death for death, can only fa-
" tisfy the furviving friends of the inju-
" red party." Something of the fame
law of retaliation was ufual amongft the
ancient Jews and Romans.

From this principle, as well as from
the high notions they have of military
glory, the young Indians fometimes fud-
denly purfue violent meafures, contrary
to the mind of their elders.

" It is, fays the fame Author, a feel-
" ing experience of the Chriftian Re-
" ligion, which alone is able to perfect

B   " their

" their good qualities, and correct that
" which is wrong in them; this is com-
" mon to them with other men; but
" what is peculiar to them is, that they
" bring fewer obftacles to this improve-
" ment, after, thro' the operation of
" grace, they have once began to believe
" in the great truths of the gofpel."

The good difpofition of the more fouthern Indians is fenfibly fet forth by De las
Cafas, Bifhop of Chapia, who fpent much
time and labour in endeavouring to preferve the Indians of New-Spain, from the
grievous oppreffion they laboured under,
in his reprefentation to the King and
Council of Spain, which, with little va-
riation, may well be applied to the natives of moft parts of the continent.
He fays, " I was one of the firft who
" went to America, neither curiofity nor
" intereft prompted me to undertake fo
" long and dangerous a voyage; the
" faving the fouls of the Heathens was
" my fole object. Why was I not per-
" mitted, even at the expenfe of my
" blood, to ranfom fo many thoufands
" of fouls who fell unhappy victims to
" avarice or luft.———It is faid, that
" barbarous executions were neceffary
" to punifh or check the rebellion of the
" Ameri-

" Americans; but to whom was this
" owing? did not thofe people receive
" the Spaniards who firft came amongft
" them, with gentlenefs and humanity?
" did they not fhew more joy, in pro-
" portion, in lavifhing treafure upon
" them, than the Spaniards did greedi-
" nefs in receiving it?————but our ava-
" rice was not yet fatisfied————tho'
" they gave up to us their land and their
" riches, we would take from them their
" wives, their children, and their liber-
" ty.————To blacken thefe unhappy
" people, their enemies affert, that they
" are fcarce human creatures————but
" it is we ought to blufh for having been
" lefs men, and more barbarous than
" they.————They are reprefented as a
" ftupid people, addicted to vice;————
" but have they not contracted moft of
" their vices from the examples of Chri-
" ftians? And as to thofe vices peculiar
" to themfelves, have not the Chriftians
" quickly exceeded them therein? Ne-
" verthelefs it muft be granted, that the
" Indians ftill remain untainted with ma-
" ny vices, ufual amongft the Europe-
" ans; fuch as ambition, blafphemy,
" treachery, and many like monfters,
" which have not yet took place with
                                " them;

" them; they have fcarce an idea of
" them, fo that, in effect, all the advan-
" tage we can claim, is to have more
" elevated notions of things, and our
" faculties more unfolded, and more
" cultivated than theirs.————Don't let
" us flatter our corruptions, nor volunta-
" rily blind ourfelves; all nations are
" equally free: one nation has no right
" to infringe upon the freedom of ano-
" ther: let us do towards thofe people,
" as we would have them to have done
" to us, if they had landed upon our
" fhore, with the fame fuperiority of
" ftrength. And, indeed, why fhould
" not things be equal on both fides.
" How long has the right of the ftrong-
" eft been allowed to be the balance of
" juftice. What part of the Gofpel
" gives a fanction to fuch a doctrine.
" In what part of the whole earth did the
" Apoftles and firft promulgators of
" the Gofpel, ever claim a right over the
" lives, the freedom, or the fubftance of
" the Gentiles. What a ftrange me-
" thod this of propagating the Gofpel,
" that holy law of grace, which from
" being flaves to fatan, initiates us into
" the freedom of the children of God."

To

To this pious Biſhop's teſtimony, may be added that of Page Dupart, in his Hiſtory of Louiſiana, who during a reſidence of ſixteen years, appears to have been careful in his enquiries, relating to the nature and diſpoſition of thoſe ſeveral nations ſeated in a ſpace of 1500 miles on both ſides the Miſſiſipi, with ſome of whom he was intimately converſant, whom he repreſents as generally endowed with good ſenſe, kindneſs and moderation. He tells us, " That upon
" an acquaintance with the Indians, he
" was convinced that it is wrong to de-
" nominate them Savages, as they are ca-
" pable of making a good uſe of their
" reaſon, and their ſentiments are juſt;
" that they have a degree of prudence,
" faithfulneſs and generoſity, exceeding
" that of nations who would be offended
" at being compared with them.

" No people, he ſays, are more ho-
" ſpitable and free than the Indians;
" hence they might be eſteemed an hap-
" py people, if that happineſs was not
" impeded by their paſſionate fondneſs
" for ſpirituous liquors, and the fooliſh
" notion they hold in common, with
" many profeſſing Chriſtians, of gaining
" reputation and eſteem, by their prow-

" eſs

" efs in war :" both which potent evils,
have from views of policy or intereft,
been much encouraged by their European neighbours "

From him, as alfo from fome other authors, we learn that fome of thefe nations
appear but little inclined to war, and there
are others who abfolutely refufe to take any
part therein, but patiently bear the hardfhips which the violence of other Indians
fubjects them to ; of which good difpofition we have had inftances amongft
ourfelves in the cafe of the Moravian Indians.

Duprat obferves upon the whole,
" That there needs but prudence and
" good fenfe, to perfuade the Indians to
" what is reafonable, and to preferve
" their friendfhip without interruption.
" He adds, We may fafely affirm that
" the differences we have had with them,
" have been more owing to us than to
" them. When they are treated info-
" lently or oppreffively, they have no lefs
" fenfibility of injuries than others. If
" thofe who have occafion to live among
" them, will have fentiments of hu-
" manity, they will meet in them with
" men."

Many

Many more authors might be quoted,
declarative of the commendable qualities
which have appeared in the Indians,
whilst uncorrupted by an intercourse with
the Europeans, and which is still the case
in the difpofition of thofe nations fituated
at a diftance from us. * This particularly

---

* Note, In a late Hiftory of the Britifh Dominions in North-America, printed in 1773, p 219,
the Author fpeaking of the Natives, fays, " The
" nearer the Indians of Canada are viewed, the
" more good qualities are difcovered in them ;
" for moft of the principles which ferve to regu-
" late their conduct : the general maxims by
" which they govern themfelves ; and the effen-
" tial parts of their character, difcover nothing
" of the barbarian."
Of the Five Nation Indians, M. Delapoterie. a
French Author, (wherein he very much agrees
with Cadwalader Colden, late prefident of New-
York) in his account of thofe Indians, fays,
" They are thought by a common miftake, to be
" mere barbarians, always thirfting for human
" blood ; but their true character is very differ-
" ent : they are indeed the fierceft and moft for-
" midable people in North America ; and at the
" fame time, as politic and judicious, as well can be
" conceived, which appears from the management
" of all the affairs they tranfact, not only with the
" French and Englifh, but likewife with almoft
" all the Indian Nations of this vaft continent.
" Speaking

larly appears from accounts left us by Jonathan Carver, who from the year 1766, to the year 1768, inclufive, vifited feveral Nations weft of the river Miffiffipi, and the upper lakes. Speaking of the general temper of the Indians fituate in thofe parts, he tells us, " They are ex-
" tremely liberal to each other, and fup-
" ply the deficiencies of their friends,
" with any fuperfluity of their own
" ————That

" Speaking of the Cherokees, and other South-
" ern Indians, page 157, he fays, Thefe Indi-
" ans look upon the end of life, to be living
" happily ; and for this purpofe, their whole
" cuftoms are calculated to prevent avarice,
" which they think imbitters life; and nothing is
" a more fevere reflection amongft them, than to
" fay, *That a man loves his own*. To prevent the
" rife and propagation of fuch a vice, upon the
" death of any Indian, they burn all that be-
" longs to the deceafed, that there may be no
" temptation for the parent to hoard up a fu-
" perfluity of arms, and domeftic conveniences
" for his children. They ftrengthen this cu-
" ftom, by a fuperftition, that it is agreeable to
" the foul of the deceafed, to burn all they leave,
" and that affliction follow thofe who ufe any of
" their goods. They cultivate no more land
" than is neceffary for their plentiful fubfiftance,
" and hofpitality to ftrangers."

" ———That governed by the plain and
" equitable laws of Nature, every one is
" remarked folely according to his de-
" ferts ; and their equality, condition,
" manners and privileges, with that con-
" ftant fociable familiarity which prevails
" thro' every Indian Nation, animates
" them with a pure and truly patriotic
" fpirit, that tends to the general good
" of the Society to which they belong.
" The Indians, he fays, are not without
" fome fenfe of Religion, fuch as proves
" that they worfhip the great Creator,
" with a degree of purity unknown to
" nations who have greater opportuni-
" ties of improvement.

" That the pleas of Indians for mak-
" ing war, are in general more rational
" and juft, than fuch as are brought by
" Europeans, in vindication of their pro-
" ceedings. To fecure the rights of
" hunting———to maintain the liberty
" of paffing thro' their accuftomed tracts,
" and to guard thofe lands which they
" confider, from a long tenure, as their
" own, againft any infringment, are the
" general caufes of thofe diffenfions
" which fo often break out between the
" Indian Nations. He agrees with
" Charlevoix, that the Indians feel in-
" juries

" juries with exquifitefenfibility; whence
" they purfue vegeance with unremitting
" ardour."

Whilft in the Indian Country, he was
inftrumental in preventing the Chipeways
and Nadoweffis Indians from profecuting
the war, which had during a courfe of
40 years, fubfifted between them. This,
the old Indians told him, they had long
wifhed to put an end to; but that their
endeavours were fruftrated by the young
warriors, of either nation, who could
not reftrain their ardour. when they met.
They faid they fhould be happy, if fome
chief of the fame pacific difpofition as
himfelf, and who poffeffed an equal degree of refolution and coolnefs, would
fettle in the country between the two nations; for by the interference of fuch a
perfon, an accommodation, which, on
their part, they fincerely defired might be
brought about. From this circumftance,
as well as what Duprat and others obferve
of the peaceable difpofition of fome of
the Indians, we may well conclude, that
fufceptible as thofe untutored people are,
to the dictates of reafon, if the profeffors
of Chriftianity had, by a proper ufe of
that fuperior knowledge they were fa-
voured with, honeftly laboured, thro'
Divine

Divine help, to acquaint them with the nature and precepts of the Gospel; to make them sensible of that universal brotherhood that loving, meek, forgiving spirit, which the precepts and example of our Saviour call for, it would have been a matter of the greatest joy both to them and us; but the reverse has happened, except in a few particular instances; the different denominations of Christians have rather added fresh fuel to this false fire, by inciting the poor Natives, when it has suited their political purpose, to violence amongst themselves, and to become parties in the wars they have waged one against another.

A disposition to misrepresent and blacken the Indians, in order to justify, or palliate the practice of unjust and cruel measures towards them, has particularly appeared in the affecting case of those Indians, denominated Moravian Indians, settled on the Muskingum, a branch of the Ohio; who have, of late, deeply suffered on account of what they thought the peaceable spirit of the Gospel required of them. A true representation of the state and disposition of those Indians, as well as an account of this deplorable transaction, drawn from the account given

en

en by the survivors, appears neceffary, as well to refcue thofe innocent fufferers from the odium which has been fo un-juftly caft upon them, as to prevent ftrangers, who may come amongft us, from forming fuch erronious ideas of the Natives, as may have an influence upon the welfare of both them, and the White People.

The firft gathering of thofe Indians into a good degree of civil and religious order, was about 30 years ago, by means of one of them, named Papunhank. The place of their refidence at that time, was at Whihaloofing, on the Sufquehanna, about 200 miles from Philadelphia. In the converfation they had with fome ferious people, in a vifit to that city, about the year 1756, at a time when the province was diftreffed by the Indian war, they appeared to have a feeling fenfe of that inward change of heart which the Gofpel requires, and declared their particular difapprobation of war, and fixed refolution to take no part therein ; apprehending it to be difpleafing to the Great Being, who, as one of them expreffed it, " *Did not make men to deftroy men ;* " *but to love and affift each other.*" They held a conference with the Governor, in

in which they informed him, " That
" they remembered the old friendfhip
" which fubfifted between their Forefa-
" thers and ours; that they were great
" lovers of peace, and, had not taken
" any part in the war."

They delivered three white prifoners
which they had recovered from the other
Indians. They defired that no ftrong
drink fhould be given them, nor be fent
to their town. The fpeaker, Papunhank, appeared ferious, as under a fenfe
of the Divine Prefence, and concluded
with a folemn prayer, with which the
whole audience feemed much affected.

About 13 years paft, thefe Indians
meeting with difficulty, from an en-
creafe of White Settlers near them,
by which fpirituous liquors were brought
to their towns; they removed to the
Mufkingum, a branch of the Ohio. In
their perigrination thither, they were accompanied by fome of the Moravians,
who have long refided with them, and
by their careful attention, both to their
civil and religious concerns, never leav-
ing them, even in the times of their greateft danger and difficulty, a near and
fteady connection between them took
place.

During

During the late troubles, thefe Indians adhering to the principles they had long profeffed, abfolutely refufed to take any part in the war, notwithftanding the threats and repeated abufes they received on that account from other tribes, particularly thofe parties which paffed thro' their towns, in their way to our frontiers; whom they fometimes diffuaded from their hoftile intentions, and prevailed upon to go back again; or warned the inhabitants of their danger. This humane conduct being confidered as obftructive to the hoftile proceedings of the Tribes at war, was at length made the pretence of carrying them off. Accordingly, on the 4th of Auguft, 1781, a ftring of Wampum was fent by the Chief of the Wyondats, who refided at Sandufky, with a meffage, letting them know, He was coming with a number of warriors; but biding them be not afraid, for he was their friend. In a few days after, 220 warriors arrived, when calling a council of the head men of the three Moravian towns, they acquainted them they were come to take them away; rendering it for a reafon, " That they, and " their Indians, were a great obftruction " to them in their war-path." They returned

turned them this anfwer : " That it was " impoffible for them to remove at that " time, and leave their corn behind them, " left they and their children fhould pe- " rifh with hunger in the wildernefs." To this, the Chief of the Wyondats, at firft, feemed to attend ; but being inftigated by fome white men in their company, they perfifted in their refolution ; and after killing many of the cattle and hogs, ripping up their bedding, and committing many other outrages, on the 28th of Auguft, and Septmber, forced them from their three towns, in all between 3 and 400 perfons ; who, after a tedious journey in the wildernefs, arrived at a branch of Sandufky creek, where the body of them were ordered to remain. Some of their principal men were fent to Major Arent Schuyler De Peyfter, the Englifh Commander at fort Detroit, who commended them, as a peaceable people, and exhorted them to remain fuch ; but added, That many complaints had been made of them ; that they had given intelligence to his enemies, &c. he had fent for them ; but that his inftructions had been exceeded, in the ill-treatment they had received ; that however he would provide for them.

Thus

Thus the matter rested till the spring, 1782, when these Moravian Indians finding corn scarce and dear at Sandusky, desired liberty to return to their settlements, to fetch some of their corn, of which they had left above 200 acres standing; which when granted, many of them went, among whom were several widows with their children, some of whom had been subjected to such extreme want, as to eat the carcases of the dead cattle and horses.

When the people at and about the Monongahela, understood a number of Indians were at the Moravian towns, they gave out, that the intention of those people was, to fall upon the back inhabitants, which ought to be prevented. Whereupon about 160 men got together, and swimming their horses over the Ohio, came suddenly upon the chief Moravian town. The first person who appeared, they shot at and wounded, when coming up to him, they found he was an half Indian, son to John Bull, one of the Moravians, by an Indian woman, to whom he is regularly married; they killed and scalped him, and proceeded to the town. The Moravian Indians, who were mostly in the fields pulling corn,

corn, did not run off, as many of them might, if they had been confcious of any offence ; but came of their own accord, into the town, at the call of the white people, who at firft, exprefled friendfhip to them ; but foon after, violently feized and bound them, when the Helpers, * of whom there were five of the moft re-fpectable, in the company, and others exhorted the younger, to fubmiffion and patience ; telling them, they thought their troubles in this world, would foon be at an end, and they would be with their Saviour. They then fung and pray-ed together, till they were led out, one after the other, and inhumanly flaughter-ed ; firft the men, and then the women. Two boys, who made their efcape, relat-ed thefe particulars. One of them lay in the heap of the dead, in a houfe, and was fcalped ; but recovering his fenfes, efcaped : the other, who had hid himfelf under the floor, was an eye-witnefs of this tragic fcene, and faw the blood of

C 2   the

---

* Thefe are Indians who affift the miffiona-ries in keeping good order amongft their people, and upon occafion, give public exhortations.

the flain running in a ftream. Thefe Indians before being bound, were fo little ap-
prehenfive of being charged with guilt,
that they informed the White People, that
more of their brethren were at another
town to which they accompanied them;
who in like manner fell a facrifice with
them, to the barbarity of the whites.
The dead bodies were afterwards burned
with the houfes. Before their death,
they were alfo obliged to fhew in what
part of the woods they had concealed
their effects, when the other Indians (as
before mentioned) took them away.

Thofe at the third town having fome
intelligence of what paffed, made their
efcape. One of the Helpers, who efcaped relates, That in a conference they had
with the other Helpers, when they confidered what they fhould do in cafe of an
attack, either from the Americans, or
the Indians, who had taken part with the
Englifh, fome of whom charged them of
having, thro' the intelligence they gave
to the Virginians, been the occafion
of the flaughter of their brethren, at
Gofchaching; the refult of their conference was, "Not to go away, neverthelefs
" to leave each one to act according to the
" feeling of his own heart. He added,
" That

" That there was fo much love amongſt
" them, that he had never felt the like
" before." This is a fummary of this
dreadful tranſaction, as it is given by the
principle leader of thofe that remain.

The Account, as it ſtands in the Pennfylvania Gazette, of April 17th, 1782,
after giving an account of the incurfions
of the Indians, adds, " That the peo-
" ple being greatly alarmed, and having
" received intelligence that the Indian
" towns, on the Muſkingum, had not
" moved as they had been told———a
" number of men properly provided, col-
" lected and rendevoufed on the Ohio,
" oppofite the Mingo Bottom, with a
" defign to furprife the above towns
" ———160 men fwam the river, and
" proceeded to the towns on the Muf-
" kingum, where the Indians had col-
" lected a large quantity of provifions
" to fupply their war-parties. They ar-
" rived at the town in the night, undif-
" covered, attacked the Indians in their
" cabbins, and fo completely furprifed
" them, that they killed and fcalped
" upwards of 90, but a few making
" their efcape, about 40 of which were
" warriors, the reſt old women and chil-
" dren. About 80 horfes fell into their
" hands,

" hands, which they loaded with the
" plunder, the greateſt part furrs and
" ſkins; and returned to the Ohio,
" without the loſs of one man."

It is alledged, in vindication of this
deliberate maſſacre, that 40 of thoſe Indians were warriors, preparing to attack
our frontiers; but this aſſertion contra-
dicts it ſelf: for had it been the caſe, it
is not likely they would have brought
their wives, with the widows, and 34
children, who were ſlain with them, or
have ſuffered them with themſelves, to be
thus murdered, without making the leaſt
reſiſtance, or hurt to their murderers.

Soon after the death of theſe Indians,
about 500 men, probably encouraged by
this eaſy conqueſt aſſembled at the old Min-
gos on the weſt ſide of the Ohio, and being
equipped, on horſeback, ſet on for Sanduſky, where the remaining part of the
Moravian Indians reſided, in order to
deſtroy that ſettlement, and other Indian
towns in thoſe parts; but the Wyandots,
and other Indians, having ſome knowledge of their approach, met them near
Sanduſky, when an engagement enſued,
in which ſome of the aſſailants were killed, and ſeveral taken priſoners, amongſt
whom was the Commander Col. Craw-
ford,

ford, and his fon-in-law. The Col. the Indians put to a cruel death, and killed the other, with other prifoners.

Doubtlefs the cruelty exercifed on the Col. and the death of the prifoners taken at Sandufky, was, in a great meafure, owing to the murder of the peaceable Moravian Indians, at which they expreff-ed much difpleafure.

This grievous tranfaction appears in a yet more afflictive point of view, when it is confidered, that tho' many threats had been thrown out againft thofe Indi-ans, both by the Englifh and Ameri-cans, * yet they took no ftep for their fe-curity,

---

* As the Wyondat King in his Speech told them, " My coufins, you Chriftian Indians, in " Gnadenhutten, Shoenbrun and Salem, I am " concerned on your account, as I fee you live " in a dangerous fituation. Two mighty and " angry Gods ftand oppofite to each other, with " their mouths wide open, and you ftand be-" tween them, and are in danger of being crufh-" ed by the one or the other of them, or both, " and crumbled with their teeth." To which the Chriftian Indians anfwered, Uncle, &c. &c. you Shawanees our Nephews——We have hi-therto not feen our fituation fo dangerous as not to ftay here. We live in peace with all mankind, and

curity, trufting in the care of Heaven, and the protection of the government, under which they had lived many years with due fubmiffion. But fuch is the corrupting nature of war, that it gradually hardens the heart, to a fearful degree of infenfibility. Yet furely a time of roufing muft come, when, if not given up to obduracy, equal to their delufion, the blood of thefe innocent people will be heavy upon all concerned in the fhedding of it.

We cry out againft Indian cruelty; but is any thing which Indians have done, (all circumftances confidered) more inconfiftent with juftice, reafon, and humanity, than the murder of thofe Moravian Indians ; a peaceable, innocent people, whofe conduct, even when under the fcalping-knife, evidenced a dependance on Divine Help for fupport, as much becoming Chriftians, as their fufferings in fupport of their religious principles, and

---

and have nothing to do with the war. We defire and requeft no more, than that we may be permitted to live in peace and quiet——We will preferve your words and confider them——and fend you, Uncle, an anfwer.

and their fidelity to the government had before manifefted them to be our fpecial friends.

In vindication of this barbarous tranf-action, endeavours have been ufed, to make us believe, that the whole race of Indians are a people prone to every vice, and deftitute of every virtue ; and with-out a capacity for improvement. What is this but blafphemoufly to arraign the wifdom of our Creator, and infinuate, that the exiftence He has given them, is incompatible with his moral government of the world. But this muft be admitted to make way for the propofal of endea-vouring the univerfal extirpation of In-dians from the face of the earth. Such, alas ! is the manner in which too many of the pretended followers, of the meek and fuffering Saviour of the world, would fulfil the prophecy concerning him, " *That he fhall have the Heathen for his* " *inheritance, and the uttermoft Parts of* " *the earth for his poffeffion.*" And who himfelf declared, " *That he came not to* " *deftroy mens' lives, but to fave them;*" and when fainting in his laft agony, un-der mockery and derifion, conceived at once a prayer, and an apology for his murderers: " *Father, forgive them, they* " *know*

" *know not what they do.*" Now fo far as we know the prevailance of this fpirit of love and forgivenefs, over the pride and wrath of our hearts, fo far are we the difciples and followers of Chrift; and fo far only, can we truly pray for, and witnefs the coming of His kingdom: and on the other hand, fo far as we are fubject to a vindictive and unforgiving fpirit, fo far we are in a ftate of alienation from God, and reprobate concerning a true faith in the Lord Jefus Chrift, which works only by love, to the purifying of the heart from every difpofition of a contrary nature. Was this diftinction always obferved in our religious . difcriminations of mankind, we fhould get thro' abundance of frivolous and fuperficial prejudices which divide the Chriftian World, and be convinced, that it is not the colour of our fkins, outward circumftances or profeffion, but the ftate and temper of the mind and will, which makes us Jews or Gentiles; Chriftians or Heathens; Elect or Reprobate, in the fight of God. That this change of heart is the fure effect of the coming of Chrift's kingdom, was evidenced in many of thofe Indians, whofe cafe is here reprefented; who, by yield-
ing

ing to the operations of Divine Grace, were brought to an entire reformation of mind and manners. That favage feroci-ty, with all thofe dazzling notions of ho-nour, to be gained from the deftruction of mankind, fo natural to the fallen fons of Adam, have gradually melted away in thefe Indians, into a frame of meek-nefs, humility and love, which fup-ported them in that lamb-like fubmiffion, under that remarkable fucceffion of trials and afflictions which was permitted to at-tend them; whereby many of them are at length put beyond the reach of enmi-ty.

We are told by a late Author, who appears zealous for the extirpation of all Indians, " *That for a keg of whiſkey,* " *you might induce any Indian to murder* " *his wife, children and beſt friend.*" That this is not a juft character of Indi-ans, all, who are acquainted with that people, can teftify: yet there are, doubt-lefs, ill-difpofed people amongft them, as well as amongft us, who under the dread-ful power of ftrong drink, (which has an uncommon bad effect on them) may be led into the greateft enormities. Never-thelefs, as has been mentioned, impar-tial men, who from good views, have

vifited

vifited or refided with them, reprefent them in a very different light: as Charlevoix, and other French and Spanifh Authors: John Elliott, Thomas Mayew; John Sergeant, in New-England; David Brainard and others in the Jerfeys; and more lately the Moravians in different parts. Thefe have fpent much time and labour for the civil and religious improvement of the Natives, in which they all exprefled fatisfaction and comfort.

And it is worthy of peculiar notice, that in the wars the Indians have waged upon our frontiers, there has fcarce been an inftance of any of thofe Indians, who had made a ferious profeffion of the Chriftian Religion, having been concerned in the barbarous eruptions againft us.*

Thefe

---

*Neal, p. 30, 2d. vol. fays, "There is one thing "which deferves to be taken notice of; that is, "the unfhaken fidelity of the Indian Converts, "during the whole courfe of the war, whom nei- "ther perfuafion nor threatnings of their coun- "trymen, could draw from their allegiance to "the Englifh. The government had a watchful "eye upon them at firft, and the mob being in- "cenfed againft Indians, could hardly be re- "ftrained from facrificing the Converts to their "fury."   The

Thefe have generally put themfelves under the protection of their feveral governments ; as former inftances in New-England, and the inftance of the Moravian
Indians, both in the former, and late
war, will undoubtedly evince.

The people of Pennfylvania, and New-
Jerfeys, as has been already noted, have
had full opportunity to experience the
good difpofition and kindnefs of the Indians, fo long as they were treated with
juftice and humanity, as particularly appears from the many ftriking inftances of
probity, gratitude and beneficence, on
record, at a time when the difparity of
their numbers was fo great, that they
might have eafily deftroyed the fettlers,
had

The fame Author obferves, That the government was fo well fatisfied with the fidelity of the
Indians, that inftead of difarming them, as was
defired, the Indians on Martha's Vineyard, who
were twenty to one in number to the White
People, continued fo faithful to their engagements, that they were fupplied with all forts of
ammunition, and the defence of the Ifland com-
mitted to their care ; and fo faithful were they to
their truft, that all people that landed upon the
Ifland, during the courfe of the war, were, without diftinction, brought before the Governor.

had they been fo minded. But fo far were they from molefting them, that they were rather as nurfing fathers to them; granting them ample room for fettlements; freely affifting them with the means of living, at eafy rates; manifefting, thro' a long courfe of years, a ftrict care and fidelity in obferving their treaties, and fulfilling their other engagements; which there is the greateft reafon to conclude would ftill be the cafe, in every part of the continent, if the fame equitable and kind meafures were purfued.

Upon the whole, it is a matter of undoubted perfuafion, with impartial people, who have been converfant with Indians, that if their dipofitions and natural powers are duly confidered, they will be found to be equally with our own, capable of improvement in knowledge and virtue, and that the apparent difference between us and them, is chiefly owing to our different ways of life, and different ideas of what is neceffary and defirable, and the advantage of education, which puts it in our power to glofs over our own conduct, however evil; and to fet theirs, however defenfible, in the moft odious point of light.

Much

Much of th€ir blamable conduct, now
complained of, is certainly imputable to
a long continued train of fraudulent and
corrupt practices, in our intercourle with
them, efpecially, the fatal introduction
of ftrong drink, of which they have often complained, * and defired it might
not

* At the treaty at Carlifle, in 1753, the Indians fay, " The Rum ruins us. We beg you.
" would prevent its coming in fuch quantities,
" We delire it may be forbidden, and none fold
" in the Indian country; but that if the Indians
" will have any, they may go amongft the in-
" habitants, and deal with them. When thefe.
" Whifkey traders come, they bring 30 or 40
" Kegs, and put them before us, and make us
" drink, and get all the fkins that fhould go to
" pay the debts we have contracted, for goods
" bought of the fair trader; and by this means,
" we not only ruin ourfelves, but them too.
" The wicked whifkey fellers, when they have
" once got the Indians in liquor, make them fell
" their very clothes from their backs. In fhort,
" if this practice be continued, we muft be ine-
" vitably ruined. We moft earneftly, therefore,
" befeech you to remedy it."
We find an early record, in the Hiftory of New-
Jerfey to the credit of the people of that day,
That at a conference they held with the Indians,
where 3 Kings or Chiefs were prefent, the fpeaker
expreffed

not be brought amongſt them, by which
inſtead of allaying the ferment of corrupt nature, by a good example, and the
good inſtruction, which our ſuperior
knowledge would enable us to give them,
too many have been inſtrumental in work-
ing them up to a ſtate of diſtraction,
which when it has burſt forth in vengeance
upon ourſelves, is made a pretence for
deſtroying them, as tho' they were whol-
ly the aggreſſors.

That Indians may be tempted or provoked to the perpetration of great evils,
by the intemperate love and uſe of ſtrong
liquors,

───────────────────

expreſſ d himſelf to the following effect: "Strong
"liquors were ſold to us by the Sweeds and by
"the Dutch; theſe people had no eyes, they
"did not ſee it was hurtful to us; that it made
"us mad. We know it is hurtful to us. Ne-
"vertheleſs, if people will ſell it to us, we are
"ſo in love with it, that we cannot forbear; but
"now there is a people come to live amongſt us,
"that have eyes; they ſee it to be for our hurt;
"they are willing to deny themſelves the profit,
"for our good. Theſe people have eyes, we are
"glad ſuch a people are come, we muſt put it
"down by mutual conſent. We give theſe 4
"belts of wampum———to be a witneſs of this
"agreement we make with you; and would
"have you tell it to your children."

liquors, is eafily conceived ; but whether they, who, to gratify the cravings of fordid avarice, furnifh them with the intoxicating potion, and then take advantage of their fituation, to impofe upon them, and tempt them to evil, are not principally accountable, for the crimes they commit, and their confequences, is not a query worthy of their moft awful confideratton.

Had the views of the inhabitants of the colonies, been more juft and wife, and their conduct towards the Natives regulated by a benevolence worthy of the Chriftian Name, every reafonable purpofe of fettling in their country, might have been fully accomplifhed, and they at the fame time become, generally, as well civilized, as thofe few who were under the care of the Moravians, at the Mufkingum.

The accounts of the wicked policy and cruelties exercifed by the Spaniards upon their Indians, we read with horror, without confidering how far ourfelves are in a degree guilty of fomething of the fame.

How many peaceable Indians, refiding amongft us, have formerly as well as lately, been murdered, with impunity,

to fatisfy the rage of angry men, tho'
under the protection of the law, without any attonement being made. *

What deſtruction both of Indians and
others, thro' a violent infringement on
what they apprehended to be their rights.
What dreadful havock has the deſire of
gain made amongſt them, by the ſale of
ſpirituous liquors, &c. &c. Surely this
muſt be accounted for, when an inqui-
ſition for blood takes place. Indeed intereſt, as well as duty, ſhould induce the
people, in general, to endeavour the
bringing the Indians off from thoſe falſe
habits and prejudices, which are as ob-
ſtructive to their own happineſs, as they
are dangerous to ours.

To what degree of diſtreſs, a few Indians can reduce a country, let the Annals of New-England teſtify, particularly by the long and diſtreſſing wars with
the Eaſtern Tribes, † who upon the making

---

* At the Coneſtogo Manor, Lancaſter town,
and ſeveral otherinſtances.

† D. Neal, ſpeaking of the cccaſion of this
war with the Eaſtern Indians, 2d. vol. page 24,
ſays, " That the Europeans cheated the
Na-

ing a peace with them, were found to be fo fmall a number, that it occafioned the celebrated Cotton Mather, to take up the following lamentation : " *Surely* " *we had fmitten the whole army of the* " *Indians, that fought againft us, twenty-* " *three years ago, from one end of the* " *land to the other ; only there were left* " *a few wounded amongft them in the* " *eaft, and now they have rifen up, eve-* " *ry man, and have fet the whole coun-* " *try on fire. Certainly a more humbling* " *matter cannot be related. Moreover, is* " *it not a very humbling thing, that when* " *about an hundred Indians durft begin a* " *war upon all thefe populous colonies, an* " *army of a thoufand Englifh raifed, muft* " *not kill one of them all, but inftead there-* " *of, more of our foldiers perifhed by fick-* " *nefs and hardfhips, than we had ene-* " *mies in the world. Our God has hum-* " *bled*

Natives in the moft open and bare-faced man-ner imaginable, and treated them like flaves. The Indians were not infenfible of this ufage; but were afraid to do themfelves juftice, till they heared that all New-England was involved in a bloody war, when they plainly told the Englifh, they would bear their infults no longer."

" *bled us. Is it not a very humbling*
" *thing, that when the number of our ene-*
" *mies afterwards increasing, yet an hand-*
" *ful of them should, for so many sum-*
" *mers together, continue our unconquered*
" *spoilers, and put us to such vast charges,*
" *that if we would have bought them for*
" *an hundred pounds a head, we should*
" *have made a saving bargain of it.*
" *Our God has humbled us.*" *

What an inftructive leffon may the
rulers of government, and the people,
gather from this pathetic lamentation;
how ought it to induce us diligently to labour for the maintenance of Peace and
Friendfhip with all our Indian neighbours.

How ought we to look up to God, the
common Father of the family of mankind, requefting he would enable us to
fow the feeds of Benevolence and Mercy, carefully avoiding thofe of War and
Deftruction.†

                                                It

---

* Hutchinfon, vol. 2, p. 4, fays, "The province
of Maffachufetts, in the courfe of fixty years,
hath been at greater expence, and hath loft more
of its inhabitants, than all the other colonies
upon the continent."

† Ibid. page 307. " Every perfon almoft, in
                                                the

It was, very probably, the want of such a care in the people of New-England, particularly in the lamentable destruction of the Pequot Indians, tho' perpetrated many years before, which produced the grievous crop of calamity and diftrefs here complained of; for however time and changes may veil paft tranfactions, and remove them from fight, and the remembrance of men, yet they will remain, as prefent, in the view of *Divine Purity*; and whilft unrepented of, will, tho' covered, as with dirt and drofs, remain as engraven on a rock, which when the overflowing ftream prevails, and that time of general inquiry, comes, when fecret things fhall be revealed, will appear as a teftimony againft tranfgreffors.

The Annals of New-England informs us, that the firft fettlers met with kind treatment from the Natives, even when they were few, and fo fickly, that in the firft winter, one half of their number died.

Hutchinfon,

---

the two colonies, had loft a relation or near friend."

Hutchinfon, obferves, " *That the Natives fhewed courtefy to the Englifh, at their firft arrival; were hofpitable, and made fuch as would eat their food, welcome to it, and readily inftructed them in the planting and cultivating the Indian Corn. Some of the Englifh who loft themfelves in the woods, and muft otherwife have perifhed with famine, they relieved and conducted home.*"

It was about fifteen years after, when the fettlement on the Connecticut river, was making fpeedy advances towards the country of the Pequots, that differences arofe between thofe Indians and the Englifh ; fome traders were killed, whether thro' the fault of the Indians, or White People, is uncertain, as each blamed the other ; the Indians, however, fhewed a great defire to maintain peace between them and the Englifh, for which purpofe Neal obferves, " *They twice fent deputies to Bofton, with prefents,*" which might with patience and forbearance, thro' the blefling of God, have been improved ; but the Englifh infifting on the delivery of the perfons concerned, which the Indians delaying to comply with, perhaps for want of power, the Englifh

fell

" *fell upon them, flew feveral, firing their*
" *wigwams, and fpoiling their corn, &c.*"
which enraged the Indians to fuch a degree, that, giving up their endeavours
for peace, they attacked the fort on Connecticut river; flew feveral perfons; and
carried away two maidens, who were afterwards returned. Upon this, the different New-England governments concluded to unite their forces, to deftroy
thofe Indians; which was fo effectually
done, that Captain Underhill, who was
a principal Commander in that expedition, in his book intitled *News from America,* page 2, tells us, " *Thofe Indians,*
" *the Pequots, were drove out of their*
" *country, and flain, by the fword, to the*
" *number of fifteen hundred fouls, in the*
" *fpace of two months or lefs; fo as their*
" *country is fully fubdued, and fallen into*
" *the hands of the Englifh.*"
Hutchinfon fays, " *This was the firft*
" *action between the Englifh and Indians;*
" *the policy, as well as the morality of which,*
" he obferves, *may well be queftioned.*"
And he adds, " *The Indians have ever*
" *fhewn great barbarity to their Englifh*
" *captives; the Englifh, in too many in-*
" *ftances, have retaliated it. This has*
" *only enraged them the more. Befides,*

E   " *to*

" *to destroy women and children, for the*
" *barbarity of their husbands, cannot be*
" *easily justified. Many of the captives*
" *were sent to Bermudas, and sold for*
" *slaves.*" *

This account of the destruction of the
Pequot Indians, is by no means intended
as a reflection on the people of New-
England ; sensible, that it is now long
since many amongst them, have been
foremost in furnishing instances of the
blessing attendant on the extension of
friendly measures, and a commendable
care for the civil and religious welfare of
the Indians ; as well as they have of late
years, shewn an examplary and praise-
worthy concern for doing justice to the
oppressed Africans : but only for this
necessary purpose, that the dreadful experience of former times, may be, as
instructive cautions in our future trans-
actions

---

* Neal, page 23, observes, relating to those
Pequot Indians, " That they made a noble stand
against the united force of New-England, and
would certainly have defended their country
against the encroachment of the English, if the
Narragansets, their inveterate enemies, had not
assisted the English to destroy them."

actions with our Indian neighbours, in the feveral fettlements now likely to be made on lands belonging to them, or claimed by them. Indeed we cannot be too weighty in confidering how we lay our foundation for future happinefs or mifery ; as our Saviour's declaration will be verified often, in time, and certainly in eternity : *That as we fow we fhall reap ; and with that meafure we meet, it fhall be meafured to us again.* And altho' the children are not accountable for the iniquity of their fathers ; yet where the children are bafking and rejoicing in the eafe and plenty they enjoy thro' the fins of their fathers, as is peculiarly the cafe of thofe, who are poffeffed of eftates procured by hard meafures towards Indians, or thro' the oppreffion of the Negroes ; thefe as they rejoice in thofe poffeffions, which the S I N has produced, cannot expect otherwife than, *to be partakers in the* P L A G U E.

Upon the whole, if the peace and fafety of the inhabitants of our wide extended frontiers ; the lives and welfare of fo many innocent and helplefs people, depends on the maintenance of a friendly intercourfe with our Indian neighbours,

bours, what greater inftances of patriot-
ifm, of love to God and mankind, can
be fhewn, than to promote, to the utmoft
of our power, not only the civiiization
of thefe uncultivated people, whom Pro-
vidence has, as it were, caft under our
care; but alfo their eftablifhment, in a
pious and virtuous life. On the other
hand, what greater injury can be done to
our country, than to diffufe, amongft the
thoughtlefs part of the people, a difpofition, and promote a conduct, tending
not only to deprive us of the advantage,
which a friendly intercourfe with them
may produce ; * but by raifing their en-
mity

---

* As it is expected that meafures are now tak-
ing to procure a free communication with the In-
dianCountry, whereby an extenfive trade with the
Natives will probably take place, and which, under
proper regulation, may prove very beneficial, or
the contrary, if left to the management of the
Traders, who have generally no other view but
gain. Is it not an object worthy the peculiar notice of the different Legiflatures, that a fpecial
guard be had againft the evil confequences which
will certainly attend, if an effectual reftraint is
not laid on the introduction of fpirituous liquors,
and other abufe, amongft the Indians.

mity and wrath, expofe the country to thofe grievous calamities, which an Indian war often has, and will again, undoubtedly produce.

APPENDIX.

E 2

APPENDIX.

IN an hiftorical account of General Boquet's expedition againft the Ohio Indians, publifhed under his infpecti-on, in 1765, we meet with a lift of the fighting men of the different Indian na-... of the northe... and fouthern di-... of North-America, amounting to tion ... ufand, five hundred and eigh-ftricts ... chiefly, of fuch ... dians fifty-fix tho... e connected with in ty, confifting, ... as the French we... ere told may be Canada and Louifiana ... tters of this

This account we are th... ... ruth, be-depended upon, fo far as ma... kind can be brought near the ... ing given by a French trader of co... rs rable note, who had refided many y... amongft the Indians.

The publifher of that account, a per-fon of reputation, now in this city, who has for many years made matters relating

to

to Indians his particular ſtudy, tells us, " That ſo large a number of fighting men may ſtartle us at firſt ſight; but the account ſeems no where exaggerated, excepting only that the Calawba nation (mentioned in the liſt to be 150 gun-men) is now almoſt extinct.

In ſome nations which we are acquainted with, the account falls, even ſhort of their numbers; and ſome others do not appear to be mentioned at all, or at leaſt not by any name known to us: Such for inſtance, are the lower Creeks, of whom we have a liſt, according to their towns. In this liſt their warriors or gun-men are 1180, and their inhabitants about 6000. Thus a comparative judgment may be formed of the nations above-mentioned; the number of whoſe inhabitants will (in this proportion to the warriors, viz. five to one) be about 283000."

From the above account of the number of Indians known to us, beſides thoſe we are unacquainted with, how important muſt it appear, to every ſenſible feeling mind, that a friendly intercourſe be maintained with them, as well from our duty as Chriſtians, as the great advantage which would ariſe from a well regulated trade; and the dreadful diſtreſs and ſuf-
ferings,

ferings, which a difagreement with them might bring upon fo vaft a number of helplefs people, on our long extended frontiers. *

In

In the hiftory of the Britifh dominions in North-America, already mentioned, 2d. vol. page 68, we meet with the following inftructive obfervations: " The perpetual increafing generations of Europeans, in America, may fupply numbers that muft in the end wear out thefe poor Indian inhabitants from their Country ; but we fhall pay dear, both in blood and treafure, in the mean while, for our injuftice.

, Our frontiers, from the nature of advancing fettlements difperfed along the branchings of the upper parts of our rivers, and fcattered in the difunited valleys, amidft the mountains, muft be always unguarded and defencelefs againft the incurfions of Indians.————The farmer driven from his little cultured lot, in the woods, is loft : The Indian in the woods, is every where at home ; every bufh, every thicket, is a camp to the Indian; from whence, at the very moment when he is fure of his blow, he can rufh upon his prey. In fhort, our frontier fettlements muft ever lie at the mercy of the favages ; and a fettler is the natural prey to an Indian, whofe fole occupation is war and hunting.

To

To countries circumftanced as our colonies are, an Indian is the moft dreadful of enemies. For in a war with Indians, no force whatever, can defend our frontiers from being a conftant wretched fcene of conflagrations, and of the moft fhocking murders. Whereas on the contrary, our temporary expeditions againft the Indians, even if fuccefsful, can do them little harm. Every article of their property is portable, which they always carry with them ; and it is no great matter of diftrefs to an Indian, to be driven from his dwelling ground, who finds a home in the firft place he fits down upon."

FINIS,